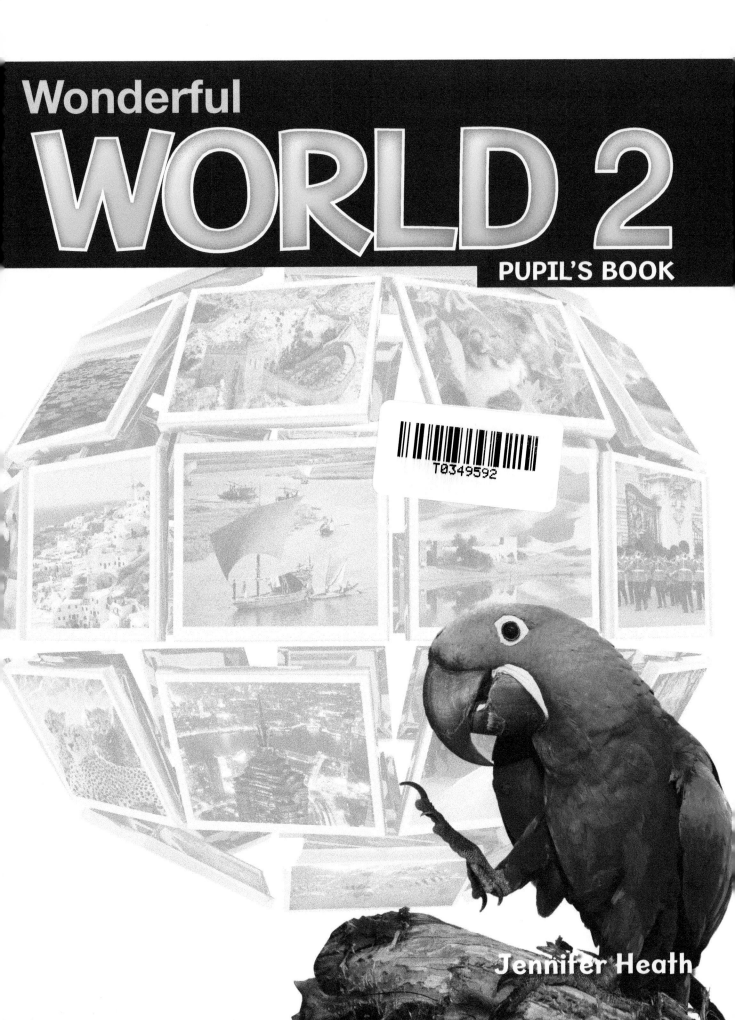

Wonderful WORLD 2

PUPIL'S BOOK

Jennifer Heath

Contents

	Grammar	Vocabulary	Page
Hello!			4
Happy Trails! Trek and his Reporters			10
Unit 1	to be (affirmative, negative, questions and short answers)	Family and adjectives	14
Unit 2	have got (affirmative, negative, questions and short answers)	Objects and animals	20
Unit 3	Possessive adjectives Possessive 's, Whose ...? There is ... / There are ... (affirmative, negative, questions and short answers) a / an, the	More objects, rooms of a house, prepositions of place and clothes	26
Let's remember!	Units 1-3		32
Fun and Games			34
Unit 4	Present Continuous (affirmative, negative, questions and short answers) Who ...? What ...?	Sports, verbs, months of the year and camping words	38
Unit 5	can (affirmative, negative, questions and short answers) must (affirmative and negative) Imperative Let's	More verbs and adjectives, adverbs, library words and ordinal numbers (1st–10th)	44
Unit 6	some / any How much / How many ...? Object pronouns	Food and drink and numbers 20-100	50
Let's remember!	Units 4-6		56
Fun and Games			58

	Grammar	Vocabulary	Page
Unit 7	Present Simple (affirmative, negative, questions and short answers)	Prepositions of time, jobs, telling the time, more verbs and adjectives	62
Unit 8	Adverbs of frequency (always, often, sometimes, never) Comparatives, Superlatives	Weather words, more objects and adjectives	68
Unit 9	to be Past Simple (affirmative, negative, questions and short answers)	Places, dinosaurs, cavemen and more adjectives	74
Let's remember!	Units 7-9		80
Fun and Games			82
Unit 10	Past Simple (affirmative – regular and irregular verbs, negative)	More verbs, history and nationalities	86
Unit 11	Past Simple (questions and short answers) be going to (affirmative and negative)	Directions and nature	92
Unit 12	be going to (questions and short answers) Future Simple (affirmative and negative)	Holidays and travel	98
Let's remember!	Units 10-12		104
Fun & Games			106
Play 1	Cinderella		108
Play 2	Aladdin		110
Halloween			112
New Year			114
May Day			116
Masks			119

Hello!

A is for 🍎 and 🧒 is for **B**.

C is for 🐱 and 🐶 is for **D**.

🥚, 🪰 and 👧 are for **E**, **F** and **G**.

🎩 and ⛺ are for **H** and **I**.

🏺, 🤴 and 🦎 are for **J**, **K** and **L**.

☀️ and 🌙 are for **M** and **N**.

1 is for **O** and **P** is for 🦜.

🧵 is for **Q** and **R** is for 🤖.

🐛 and 🌳 are for **S** and **T**.

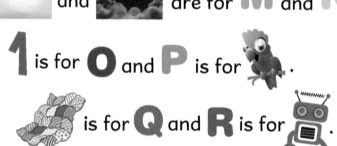

U is in 🚌 and 🚐 is for **V**.

🐋, 🦊 and 💦 are for **W**, **X**, **Y**.

Here's **Z** and 🦓 and a big GOODBYE!

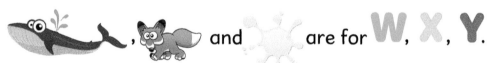

B Write.

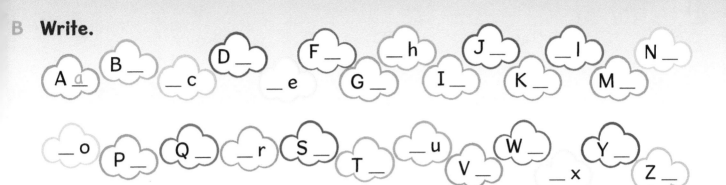

A a   B _   _ c   D _   _ e   F _   G _   _ h   I _   J _   K _   _ l   M _   N _

_ o   P _   Q _   _ r   S _   T _   _ u   V _   W _   _ x   Y _   Z _

C Write.

black   blue   brown   green   orange   pink   purple   red   white   yellow

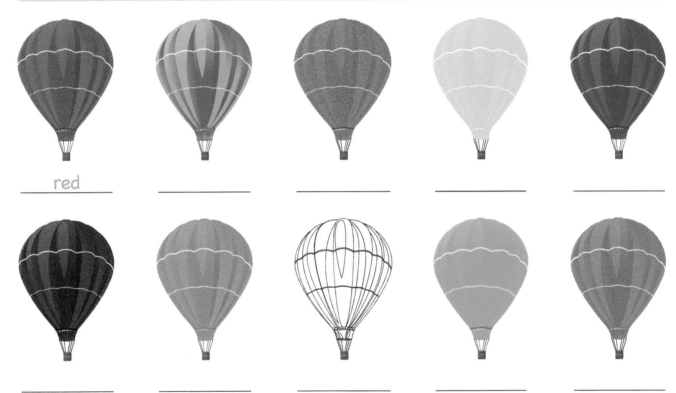

red   _____   _____   _____   _____

_____   _____   _____   _____   _____

D Listen and say.

Hello. I'm Amber. What's your name?

Hi. My name's Chris.

Hello!

E Write.

Friday   Monday   Saturday   Sunday
Thursday   Tuesday   Wednesday

1 Monday
   watch TV

2 _____
   play football

3 _____
   have maths lesson

4 _____
   cook

5 _____
   play basketball

6 _____
   Tessy's birthday

7 _____
   see Grandma and Grandpa

F Listen and say.

How are you?

Fine, thanks.

G Match.

eight
five
four
nine
one
seven
six
ten
three
two

H Write.

 ele _v_ e _n_

12 _ we _ ve

13 th _ rt _ en

14 fo _ r _ een

15 fi _ tee _

16 _ ix _ een

17 se _ e _ teen

18 e _ g _ teen

19 nin _ te _ n

20 t _ ent _

I Listen and say.

How old are you?

I'm eleven.

Hello!

J Write.

öne

penguin	
baby	
dress	
tomato	
foot	

lots

penguins	
children	
beaches	
men	

K Count and write.

1 _____ seven trees _____

2 _____

3 _____

4 _____

5 _____

6 _____

7 _____

8 _____

L **Write This, That, These or Those.**

1 _____This_____ is a
beautiful flower.

2 _____ boys
are my friends.

3 _____ is
Dad's car.

4 _____ computer
game is cool.

5 _____ apples
are yummy!

6 _____ whale
is fantastic!

M **Sing.**

What's your name?
What's your name?
Are you John or Tom or Shane?
What's your name?
What's your name?
Are you Ann or Pam or Jane?

Boys and girls,
How are you?
Fine, thanks!
Fine, thanks!

How are you?

How old are you?
How old are you?
Are you nine or ten or two?
How old are you?
How old are you?
Are you twelve or twenty-two?

B Find and stick.

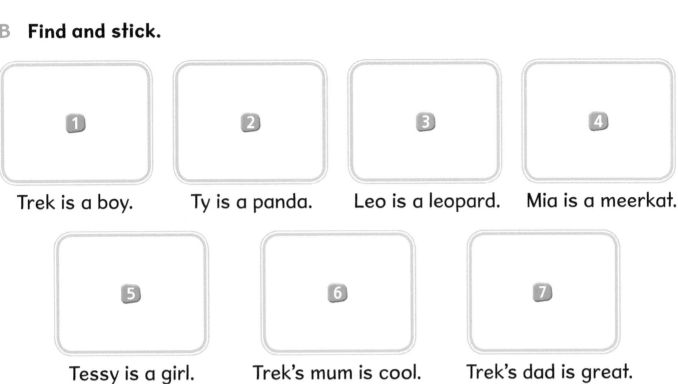

Trek is a boy. Ty is a panda. Leo is a leopard. Mia is a meerkat.

Tessy is a girl. Trek's mum is cool. Trek's dad is great.

C Write.

1 His name's ___Trek___ .

2 This is _____ .

3 This is _____ .

4 This is _____ .

5 My name's _____ .

D Sing.

Happy Trails! Happy Trails!
Hello everybody at
Happy Trails! Happy Trails!
Hello everybody at Happy Trails.

We're Trek's reporters.
Party! Party! Party!
We're Trek's reporters.
Come on, everybody!

Mia, Ty and Leo too.
Party! Party! Party!
Mia, Ty and Leo too.
Come on, everybody!

Morocco

1 Happy Trails in Morocco

 sand   stars   tea   email   camel

A Listen and read.

1 A DVD from Morocco, Mum. I've got an email too.

2 We're in the Sahara. The sand is very hot!

Look! It's Dina!

She's the new reporter.

3 Hello! Hello! Welcome to Morocco!

Oh!

4 Hi. I'm Hassan. This is tea.

Thanks, Hassan.

5 Cool camels!

Bye, Hassan.

6 Look at the stars! They're beautiful!

Look at Ty!

B Look and learn.

I'm Amber.
He's Chris.

We're friends.

I'm
you're
he/she/it's
we/you/they're

Remember!
'm = am
're = are
's = is

She's a reporter.
They're camels.

C Write am, are or is.

1 You __are__ my best friend.
2 Hello. I _____ Dennis.
3 It _____ a fox.
4 They _____ teachers.
5 The desert _____ hot.
6 The stars _____ fantastic.

Say it!

Listen and say.
email
chair

Read and listen.
It hasn't got hair,
but it's got a tail.

D Sing.

Trails in the sand.
It's hot! It's hot!
Trails in the sand.
It's hot! It's hot!

A tent in the desert.
Tea for you and me!
A tent in the desert.
Tea for you and me!

Riding on a camel.
Up and down we go!
Riding on a camel.
Up and down we go!

1 Alice and Jack are cousins.

aunt   uncle   cousin   forest

A Listen and read.

This is Alice. She's from America. She's with her cousin, Jack. They're in the Dixie National Forest. They're having fun. They love snow!

That's Jack's mum. She is Alice's aunt. She's very happy. Jack's dad is Alice's uncle. He isn't her dad's brother. He's her mum's brother.

B **Tick (✔) Yes or No.**

		Yes	No
1	Alice is with her brother.	☐	✔
2	Jack is Alice's cousin.	☐	☐
3	Jack and Alice are in a park.	☐	☐
4	Alice's mum is in the photo.	☐	☐
5	Jack's dad is Alice's uncle.	☐	☐

16

C Look and learn.

She isn't Amber!

I'm not
you aren't
he/she/it isn't
we/you/they aren't

I'm not in the photo.
They aren't sad.

Remember!
'm not = am not
aren't = are not
isn't = is not

D Write.

1 She's my aunt.   _She isn't my aunt._

2 I'm Kate.   _____

3 He's my cousin.   _____

4 My uncles are nice.   _____

5 You're from England.   _____

6 It's a cool photo.   _____

E Listen and number.

☐   1   ☐   ☐   ☐

F Say.

She isn't my mum.
She's my aunt.
Her name is Maria.

17

1 It's a photo album.

 cute ugly   photo album   twins   old young   handsome

A Read.

Sally: What's this?

Vicky: It's a photo album.

Sally: Is she your mum?

Vicky: No, she isn't! She's my grandma. She's old.

Sally: Is he your brother?

Vicky: Yes, he is. He's young. He's two.

Sally: He's cute.

Vicky: These are my sisters.

Sally: Are they twins?

Vicky: Yes, they are.

Sally: They're beautiful.

Vicky: And this is my uncle. He's handsome.

Sally: Yes, but his dog is ugly!

Vicky: No, it isn't! It's cute.

B Match.

1 She's old.
2 He's cute.
3 They're beautiful.
4 He's handsome.
5 It isn't ugly.

C Look and learn.

Is your pet cute?

Yes, it is.

Am I ...?
Yes, I am. / No, I'm not.

Is he/she/it ...?
Yes, he/she/it is. / No, he/she/it isn't.

Are we/you/they ...?
Yes, we/you/they are. / No, we/you/they aren't.

Are they brothers? Yes they are.
Is she old? No, she isn't.

D Write.

1 Is he handsome?
   Yes, he is.

3 Are they young?
   _____

2 Are you old?
   _____

4 Are you twins?
   _____

E Say.

My mum is young.
She's beautiful.
My uncle is old.
He's handsome.

F Draw and write.

My _____ .

_____ .

My _____ .

_____ .

acrobat   slippers   lamp   teapot   rug

amazing
Help!
here
I've got an idea!

A Listen and read.

1

This is my favourite city.

It's beautiful here.

2

Welcome to my shop.

Nice slippers!

And great bags!

3

Look. I've got a bag.

I've got a teapot.

I've got a lamp.

I've got slippers and a rug.

4

I've got an idea! Come on!

5

Look! Here is the market.

6

Those acrobats are amazing!

What's this?

Mia! No!

7

Help! A snake!

What ...?

B Look and learn.

I've got a snake.

Help!

I/you/we/they've got
he/she/it's got

Remember!
've got = have got
's got = has got

She's got a nice bag.
You've got red jacket.

C Write 've got or 's got.

1 I _____'ve got_____ beautiful slippers.
2 She _____ a teapot.
3 You _____ a big bag.
4 They _____ an old lamp.
5 He _____ new rug.
6 We _____ an idea!

D Listen and tick (✔) Yes or No.

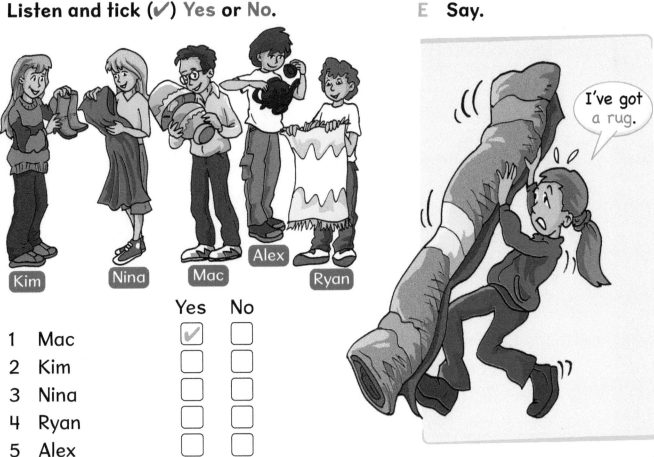

Kim   Nina   Mac   Alex   Ryan

	Yes	No
1 Mac	✔	
2 Kim		
3 Nina		
4 Ryan		
5 Alex		

E Say.

I've got a rug.

21

2 Pets are fun.

 canary goldfish kitten puppy garden swing

Lesson 2

A Listen and read.

Lots of children have got pets. Pets are fun. Some children have got cats or kittens, dogs or puppies, or goldfish.

This is Clare. She's got three pets. She's sitting on a swing with Kitty in the garden. Kitty is her brown and white kitten. She's got a goldfish and a canary too. Canaries are small yellow birds. She likes puppies, but she hasn't got a puppy.

B Match.

1 It's brown and white.
2 Clare's got a goldfish.
3 Canaries are small birds.
4 Clare hasn't got a puppy.

C Look and learn.

I haven't got a dog!

Ha! Ha!

I/you/we/they haven't got
he/she/it hasn't got

Remember!
haven't = have not
hasn't = has not

She hasn't got a goldfish.
We haven't got flippers.

D Write.

1 I've got a puppy.
   I haven't got a puppy.

2 He's got a canary.
   _____

3 She's got a goldfish.
   _____

4 My mum has got a small car.
   _____

5 You've got a kitten.
   _____

6 They've got two pets.
   _____

Say it!

Listen and say.
name
nice

Read and listen.
Jane is my name and
I like white cats.

E Sing.

Purr like a kitten.
Purr purr purr!
Miaow like a cat.
Miaow miaow miaow!

Yap like a puppy.
Yap yap yap!
Bark like a dog.
Bark bark bark!

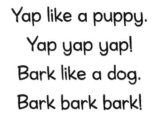

Tweet like a canary.
Tweet tweet tweet!
Chirp like a bird.
Chirp chirp chirp!

Come on pets!
Purr purr! Miaow miaow!
Yap yap! Bark bark!
Tweet tweet! Chirp chirp!

2 Has it got fur?

leopard   fur   butterfly   wing   rhino   horn   snail   shell

A Do the quiz.

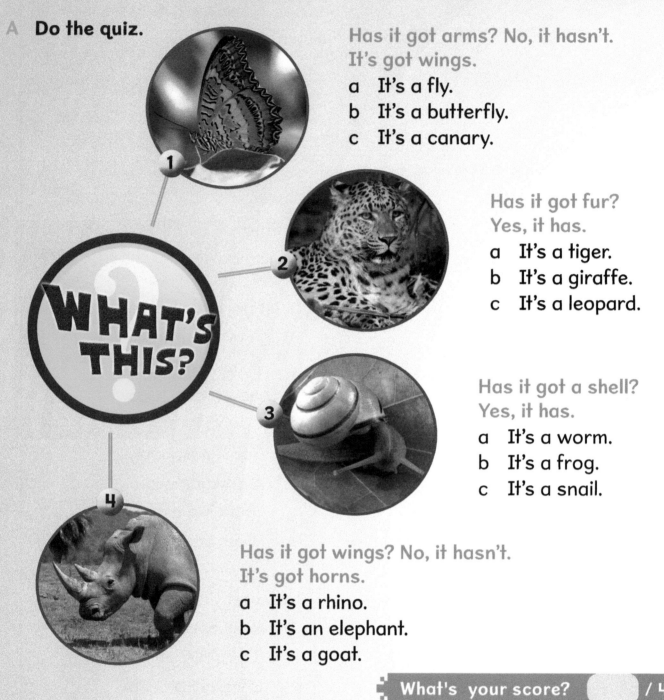

Has it got arms? No, it hasn't.
It's got wings.
a It's a fly.
b It's a butterfly.
c It's a canary.

Has it got fur?
Yes, it has.
a It's a tiger.
b It's a giraffe.
c It's a leopard.

Has it got a shell?
Yes, it has.
a It's a worm.
b It's a frog.
c It's a snail.

Has it got wings? No, it hasn't.
It's got horns.
a It's a rhino.
b It's an elephant.
c It's a goat.

What's your score? ____ / 4

B Write.

leopard   butterfly   rhino   snail

1 It's got wings.   __butterfly__
2 It's got fur.   _____
3 It's got a shell.   _____
4 It's got a big horn.   _____

24

C Look and learn.

Have you got wings?

Yes, I have.

Have **I** got ...?
Yes, **I** have.
No, **I** haven't.

Have **you** got ...?
Yes, **you** have.
No, **you** haven't.

Has **he/she/it** got ...?
Yes, **he/she/it** has.
No, **he/she/it** hasn't.

Have **we** got ...?
Yes, **we** have.
No, **we** haven't.

Have **you** got ...?
Yes, **you** have.
No, **you** haven't.

Have **they** got ...?
Yes, **they** have.
No, **they** haven't.

Has a zebra got a horn? No, it hasn't.
Have you got a garden? Yes, we have.

D Match.

1 Have giraffes got long necks?
2 Have you got a pet?
3 Has it got a shell?
4 Has John got a goldfish?
5 Has she got wings?
6 Have ostriches got fur?

No, it hasn't.
Yes, they have.
Yes, he has.
Yes, I have.
No, they haven't.
No, she hasn't.

E Say.

What animal am I?

Have you got fur?

Yes, I have. You're a leopard!

F Draw and write.

I've got _____.
I haven't _____.
I'm a _____!

25

3 Happy Trails in Morocco

 bench
 fountain
 wall
 door
 MP3 player

tired
Time for bed.

A Listen and read.

1. We're in Rabat. This is the castle.
   It's amazing!
   Look at the walls!

2. This door is beautiful!
   This is a very old castle!

3. These are my favourite gardens.
   They're beautiful. Look! A fountain.
   A bench! I'm tired.

4. Whose MP3 player is this?
   Ouch! It's my MP3 player.
   I'm sorry, Ty.

5. Listen.
   Aah! Whose music is that?
   It's Ty's music.

6. Morocco is amazing. Dina is a great reporter.
   Time for bed, Trek!
   OK, Mum.

26

B Look and learn.

That's my MP3 player, Chris!

I	my	we	our
you	your	you	your
he	his	they	their
she	her		
it	its		

That's your toy.

Whose **scooter** is this? It's Ben's scooter.
Whose **slippers** are these? They're Jane's slippers.

Be careful!
its
it's = it is

C Circle.

1 The kings / king's castle is very big.

2 I'm Jane. This is my / her MP3 player.

3 We've got mobile phones in our / their bags.

4 Whose photo album is this? It's my sisters / sister's photo album.

5 That kitten has got a ball. Its / It's ball is red.

6 Whose books are these? They're Henry's / Henry books.

D Sing.

Say it!

Come on everybody!

My name is Ty.
I'm a reporter,
All around the world.
I report!

Deserts and camels.
Castles and walls.
Markets and slippers.
Morocco's got them all!

Listen and say.
castle
listen
climb

Read and listen.
Thomas has got a
castle on the island.

3 There are toys everywhere!

 floor toy box window near between

everywhere
messy
do homework

A Listen and read.

Joy's bedroom is very big. It's very messy too.

Joy's bed is near the window. There are lots of toy boxes under her bed. But there aren't any toys in the boxes! There are toys on the floor. There are toys between the bed and the desk. Joy's toys are everywhere!

Joy is on the floor. She's doing her homework. Are there any books and notebooks in her bedroom? Yes, there are. They're on the floor next to Joy.

B Circle.

1 Joy's bedroom isn't (small) / messy.
2 Joy has got toy boxes on / under her bed.
3 There are toys between / next to the bed and the desk.
4 Joy is playing / doing her homework.

28

C Look and learn.

Are there footballs in this shop?

No, there aren't!

There's a toy on the bench.
There are photos on the door.

There isn't an MP3 player on the desk.
There aren't any toys under the bed.

Is there ...?   Yes, there is. / No, there isn't.
Are there ...?   Yes, there are. / No, there aren't.

Remember!
There's = There is
isn't = is not
aren't = are not

D Circle.

1   There are / is three dogs near the fountain.
2   Are / Is there a toy helicopter under the chair?
3   There isn't / aren't a book between the bed and the desk.
4   Are there lots of skateboards in the shop? No, there isn't / aren't.
5   There is / are a dress on the floor.

E Listen and number.

F Say.

This is my bedroom.
There are lots of toys.
There's a nice bed.
It's near the door.

29

3 It's a girls' shop!

Lesson 3

 belt café coat gloves trousers sweater

Don't worry!
good
lunch
shopping
want

A Read.

Kerry: Look at the sky, Dad! It's a beautiful day for shopping. Oh ... here we are! My favourite shop!

Dad: Are there lots of clothes here?

Kerry: Yes ... there are coats and sweaters and trousers and skirts.

Dad: Are there any clothes for me?

Kerry: No, there aren't! It's a girls' shop!

Dad: Oh no!

Kerry: Don't worry! There's a men's shop next to it.

Dad: Good. I want a belt and gloves. Is there a café near the shop?

Kerry: Yes, there is! We can eat lunch there.

B Match.

1 Is Kerry with her mum?   No, there aren't.
2 Are there lots of clothes in Kerry's favourite shop? No, he isn't.
3 Are there any clothes for men?   No, she isn't.
4 Is Kerry's dad in the café?   Yes, there are.
5 Is the café next to the men's shop?   No, it isn't.

30

C Look and learn.

The trousers are small and the shoes are big.

This is a coat. The coat is long.
It's an old jacket.
The gloves are nice.

the sun
the moon
the sea
the sky

D Write a, an or the.

1 Look! It's _____a_____ sweater. _____The_____ sweater is red.
2 _____ trousers are new.
3 Look at _____ stars in _____ sky.
4 This is _____ nice bag.
5 I want _____ orange belt.
6 _____ black socks are very long.

E Say.

coat belt boots sweater
scarf dress shoes gloves

Look! A belt.

The belt is brown. It's short too.

F Draw and write.

This is my favourite shop.
Look! _____.
The _____
_____.

31

Let's remember!

A Find and stick.

1	2	3	4	5	6
kitten	puppy	camel	butterfly	rhino	snail

B Write.

aunt   cousin   door   floor   fur   horn
shell   twins   uncle   wall   window   wing

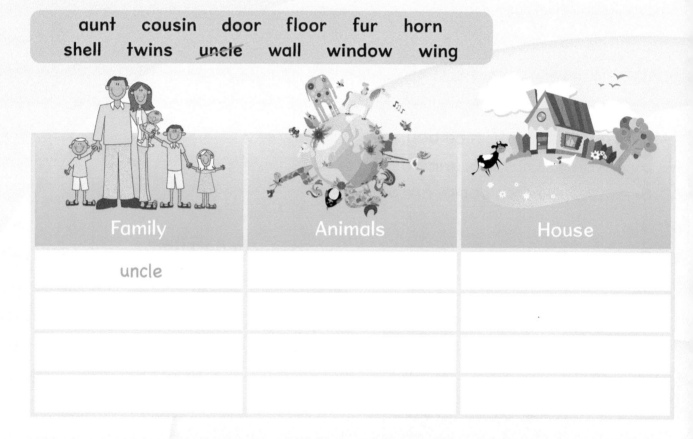

Family	Animals	House
uncle		

C Circle.

1 Wow! That young acrobat is messy / (amazing).

2 We've got a big swing / teapot in our garden.

3 There are lots of old trees in the forest / fountain.

4 My gloves are between / near the toy box.

5 It's nine o'clock, Ben. Come on! Time for bed / Don't worry!

6 I want a new belt / bench for my trousers.

7 I can't see. Where's the rug / lamp in this bedroom?

8 That baby leopard is very handsome / cute.

32

D Write.

1 My fish ____is____ orange.

2 Milly and Sally _____ old.

3 Your bedroom _____ messy!

4 Are we handsome? Yes, you _____ .

5 Is the tea hot? No, it _____ .

6 I _____ ugly! I'm beautiful.

E Write.

1 _____Have_____ they _____got_____ toys? Yes, they have.
2 An elephant _____ small ears. They're big.
3 Look! You _____ an email. It's from Tina.
4 Oh no! It's cold and I _____ a coat!
5 _____ a canary _____ fur? No, it hasn't.

F Circle.

1 (There is) / There are a snail on the wall.
2 I've got a / an idea!
3 Are there / Is there stars in the sky?
4 A / The gloves are big.
5 Is there a camel on the sand? Yes, there is / isn't.

G Circle.

1 This forest is great. (Its) / It's trees are tall.
2 I'm Mary and this is my / her aunt.
3 George and his / her sister Tina are tired.
4 We've got a photo album. Your / Our photo album is nice.
5 Whose sweater is this? It's Dad's / Dads sweater.

33

This boy and girl are cousins. They live in Alaska. They're playing in the forest now.

Quiz time!

What season is it?

a spring

b autumn

A Say.

B Sing.

You're cute.
You're handsome.
Say cheese, please!

You're cute.
You're handsome.
Say cheese, please!

You're old.
You're young.
Say cheese, please!

You're happy.
You're excited.
Say cheese, please!

CHEESE!

C Make.

35

Canada

fall   ice hockey   shout   ski   team

I'm freezing!

A Listen and read.

1 Look, Trek. The reporters are in Canada.

Cool! Thanks, Dad.

2 Hi, Trek. We're in Calgary!

3 Look at me! I'm skiing!

I'm freezing! It's cold here.

It's winter, Dina!

4 Whee ... Ahhh!

Oh no! Leo is falling!

5 Are you OK, Leo?

Look! Leo is Santa Claus!

Later ...

6 This is ice hockey. The Calgary team is red.

They're great!

7 They're winning! YES! HOORAY!

Dina is shouting!

B Look and learn.

Oh no! I'm falling!

I'm laughing
you're laughing
he/she/it's laughing
we/you/they're laughing

Remember!
win = winning
have = having

You're kicking the ball.
It's eating a carrot.

C Write.

1 You ___'re having___ (have) fun.
2 She _____ (watch) the acrobats.
3 We _____ (listen) to music on our MP3 players.
4 My brother _____ (study) in his bedroom.
5 Rick and Thomas _____ (do) their homework.
6 I _____ (play) ice hockey.

D Listen and number.

E Say.

Dad   Billy

Grandpa

Mum   Felix

Grandma

Tina

Who's sleeping?

Grandma and Grandpa

4 She's snowboarding.

Lesson 2

snowboard

January | February | March | April | May | June
July | August | September | October | November | December

A Listen and read.

month
today

Spring and summer in Canada are nice. It isn't cold. In March, April and May there are beautiful flowers everywhere. June, July and August are hot months.

In September, October and November, the trees are beautiful. They're yellow, red and brown.

It's very cold in winter. There's lots of snow in December, January and February. Men, women and children have fun in the snow. This woman isn't skiing today. She's snowboarding.

B Tick (✔) Yes or No.

	Yes	No
1 It's cold in Canada in spring.	☐	✔
2 It's hot in August.	☐	☐
3 The trees are green in November.	☐	☐
4 There's lots of snow in winter.	☐	☐
5 The woman in the photo is skiing.	☐	☐

C Look and learn.

I'm not having fun.

I'm not **standing**
you aren't **standing**
he/she/it isn't **standing**
we/you/they aren't **standing**

He isn't **dancing**.
They aren't **reading**.

D Write.

1 We ___aren't climbing___ (not climb) a tree.

2 He _____ (not swim) in the river.

3 It's Saturday. They _____ (not work).

4 My cousin _____ (not study) today.

5 I _____ (not buy) apples.

6 You _____ (not laugh).

Say it!

Listen and say.
Canada
nice

Read and listen.
In October, November and December, it's cold.

E Chant.

January, February, March.
Clap your hands for April!
May, June, July.
Stamp your feet for August!

September, October,
And November too.
Say hooray for December!
HOORAY!
Come on everybody!
Let's say hooray for all the months!
HOORAY!

Camping is fun!

camping   fire   burgers   sleep   sleeping bag   village

A Read.

stay
See you soon!

Dear Sam,

How are you? Are you staying with your grandma in the village?

I'm on holiday with Mum, Dad and my sisters. We're staying in a tent in a beautiful forest. Camping is fun! Am I sleeping in a bed? No, I'm not! I've got a sleeping bag.

My sister is cooking burgers on a fire. Yummy! Everybody is hungry!

See you soon!

Betty

Samantha Smith
10, Flower Street
New Town
NT3 456

B Circle.

1 Sam's / Betty's grandma lives in the village.
2 Betty is on holiday with Grandma / Mum and Dad and her sisters.
3 She's got a tent / forest.
4 She's sleeping in a sleeping bag / bed.
5 Betty's sister is eating / cooking burgers.
6 The burgers are hungry / yummy.

42

C Look and learn.

Are you sleeping?

Yes, I am!

Am I thinking?
Yes, I am.
No, I'm not.

Are you thinking?
Yes, you are.
No, you aren't.

Is he/she/it thinking?
Yes, he/she/it is.
No, he/she/it isn't.

Is he staying in an igloo?
No, he isn't.

Are we thinking?
Yes, we are.
No, we aren't.

Are you thinking?
Yes, you are.
No, you aren't.

Are they thinking?
Yes, they are.
No, they aren't.

Are they jumping?
Yes, they are.

D Write.

1 Are you singing? (✗)　　　　　No, we aren't.
2 Is he making a birthday cake? (✔) _____
3 Are they cooking burgers on a fire? (✔) _____
4 Is she sleeping in a sleeping bag? (✗) _____
5 Are you reading a book, Ron? (✔) _____

E Say.

What are you doing?

I'm sleeping in a sleeping bag.

F Write.

Dear _____,
I'm on holiday.
I'm staying _____.
Now I'm _____.
I'm not _____.
See _____!

_____

5 Happy Trails in Canada

Lesson 1

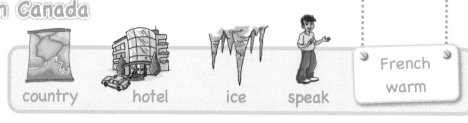

country   hotel   ice   speak   French   warm

A Listen and read.

1

Wow! I can see a big castle!

Can I watch the DVD too?

2

Canada is a nice country!

Look, Dina! Lots of snow.

3

I can't stand up!

Ouch!

4

Can you see the castle?

It's beautiful. But it's cold here.

And there's ice on the river.

5 Later ...

Wow! Everything is ice!

It's the Ice Hotel.

Bonjour.

6

Can you speak French, Dina?

Yes, I can.

It's OK. I can speak English.

7

This hotel is great!

This quilt is great! I'm warm now.

Dina is funny!

44

B Look and learn.

Ouch!

Can you run fast?

Yes, I can! Let's go!

I/you/he/she/it/we/you/they can
I/you/he/she/it/we/you/they can't

He can ride a bike.
We can't sleep.

Can I watch TV please?
Yes, you can. / No, you can't.

Remember!
can't = cannot

C Write can or can't.

We __can't__ ski.

Bonjour.

? I _____ speak French.

_____ you stand, Suzy?

No, I _____ .

I _____ swim.

_____ you see the Ice Hotel?

No, we _____ .

_____ we play in the park, Mum?

Yes, we _____ .

D Listen and circle.

1 Mia can see a hotel / castle.

2 Dina can stand on the snow / ice.

3 Leo / Ty can't run.

4 Trek can / can't watch TV.

5 Ty / Mia can speak French.

E Say.

Can you speak English?

Yes, I can.

Can you ski?

No, I can't.

45

baseball cap trainers  catch throw high fast slow

Listen and read.

number sports

Jerry loves sports. He's in the school baseball team. There are nine boys in the team. Jerry is number 32. It's his lucky number!

Look! Jerry is throwing the ball. He's got a baseball glove. He's wearing his baseball cap and his trainers too.

He must run fast. He must jump high and catch the ball. He mustn't be slow.

B Write.

1 There are nine boys in the baseball __team__ .
2 Jerry's lucky number is _____ .
3 Jerry's wearing a baseball cap and _____ .
4 He must jump _____ .
5 He mustn't be _____ .

46

C Look and learn.

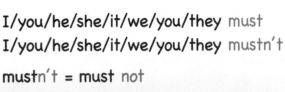

You mustn't wear shoes. You must wear trainers.

I/you/he/she/it/we/you/they must
I/you/he/she/it/we/you/they mustn't

mustn't = must not

We mustn't climb trees.

D Write must or mustn't.

1 Pupils ___must___ listen to their teachers.
2 It's time for sports. Pupils _____ wear trainers.
3 Pupils _____ eat in the classroom.
4 Pupils _____ sleep in lessons.
5 Pupils _____ shout in school.
6 Pupils _____ study.

E Sing.

It's time for sports!
Put on your shorts,
and your trainers too!

You must sit down and reach up high.
You must stand up and touch the sky.

You must run fast. You mustn't be slow.
You must jump high. There you go!

Sit down.
Stand up.
Run and jump.

Come on boys and girls!
It's time for sports!

5 Shh! Be quiet!

library   shelf

first – 1st   sixth – 6th
second – 2nd   seventh – 7th
third – 3rd   eighth – 8th
fourth – 4th   ninth – 9th
fifth – 5th   tenth – 10th

Be quiet!

A Read.

Mark: This is a great library.

Nancy: Where are the children's books?

Mark: They're on the first, second and third shelf.

Nancy: Oh look! My favourite book. *Charlie and the Chocolate Factory.*

Mark: I like Harry Potter books. I've got the fourth book.

Nancy: Is it good?

Mark: Yes, it is. Have they got the fifth book here?

Nancy: Let's look for it on that shelf.

Mark: OK. Is it the sixth book on the shelf?

Nancy: No, it isn't. Let's see. Seventh, eighth, ninth ... here it is!

Mark: It's the tenth book! Hooray!

Nancy: Ssh! Be quiet. This is a library!

B Circle.

1 *Charlie and the Chocolate Factory* is Mark's / (Nancy's) favourite book.
2 Mark / Nancy likes Harry Potter books.
3 Mark has got the fourth / fifth Harry Potter book.
4 Mark's book is the ninth / tenth book on the shelf.
5 Nancy / Mark isn't quiet.

C Look and learn.

Look! This is my favourite book!

Ssh! Don't shout!

Look!
Don't look!
Let's look at those books!

D Write.

1 at / that / look / shelf

   Look at that shelf!

2 museum / don't / in / shout / the

   _____

3 go / library / to / the / let's

   _____

4 chair / don't / on / stand / the

   _____

5 buy / let's / notebooks / some

   _____

Say it!

Listen and say.

1 – 1st	6 – 6th
2 – 2nd	7 – 7th
3 – 3rd	8 – 8th
4 – 4th	9 – 9th
5 – 5th	10 – 10th

E Say.

Don't listen to music in the library.

Read a book in the library.

be quiet   run   walk
read a book   eat   sleep
shout   listen to music

F Write.

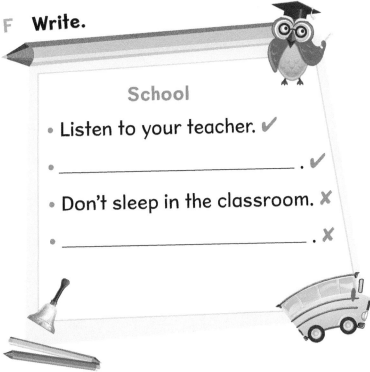

School

• Listen to your teacher. ✔

• _____ . ✔

• Don't sleep in the classroom. ✗

• _____ . ✗

6 Happy Trails in Canada

Lesson 1

grass lemonade orange juice sandwich table thirsty water waterfall

A Listen and read.

1. Welcome to Niagara Falls.
That waterfall is very big!

2. This is fun.
There's water everywhere.
Everybody is wet!

3. Let's have a picnic here.
There aren't any chairs or tables.
We can sit on the grass.

4. Are there any sandwiches?
Yes, there are.
Yummy! I love sandwiches and I'm hungry!

5. I'm thirsty. Is there any lemonade?
No, there isn't.
But we've got some orange juice.

6. Canada is fun, Trek. There's skiing here.
There's ice hockey here!
There are great hotels here.
And a lot of water!
7. Bye reporters!

50

B Look and learn.

We haven't got any orange juice.

Look! There's some orange juice in that jug.

There's some lemonade.
There isn't any lemonade.
Is there any lemonade?

We've got some lemonade.
We haven't got any lemonade.
Have we got any lemonade?

There are some sandwiches.
There aren't any sandwiches.
Are there any sandwiches?

We've got some sandwiches.
We haven't got any sandwiches.
Have we got any sandwiches?

C Write some or any.

1 There isn't _____any_____ water in the glass.
2 I've got _____ sweets in my bag.
3 Are there _____ hotels in this town?
4 Have we got _____ burgers?
5 There are _____ beautiful waterfalls here.
6 We haven't got _____ flour.

Say it!

Listen and say.
fun
computer

Read and listen.
There are hungry pupils on the bus.

D Sing.

Look at the sun,
In the sky.
Look at the birds,
Flying high.

We're having a picnic.
It's a nice day.
Sandwiches and cake,
And cool lemonade.

Look at the waterfall.
Over there.
Look at the trees.
They're everywhere!

6 How many ice creams do you eat?

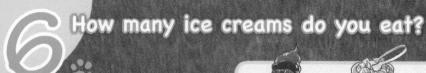

Lesson 2

ice cream   sugar

20 – twenty   60 – sixty
30 – thirty   70 – seventy
40 – forty   80 – eighty
50 – fifty   90 – ninety
100 – one hundred

A Listen and read.

Everybody loves ice creams. But are they good for you?

There's milk in ice creams and milk is good for you. But there's sugar in ice creams too. Sugar isn't good for you. How much sugar is there in one ice cream? A lot!

How many ice creams do you eat in the summer? Ten, twenty, thirty, forty or fifty? Some children eat sixty, seventy or eighty ice creams! Some children eat ninety or one hundred ice creams!

B Choose a or b.

1   Is there milk in ice creams?
   a Yes, there is.   b No, there isn't.

2   Is sugar good for you?
   a Yes, it is.   b No, it isn't.

3   Is there a lot of sugar in one ice cream?
   a Yes, there is.   b No, there isn't.

C Look and learn.

How many ...?
ice creams
sandwiches
oranges

How much ...?
lemonade
sugar
chocolate

How many cakes are there? Two.
How much water is there? A lot.

D Write How many or How much.

1 _How many_ children are playing in the park?
2 _____ chocolate do you eat every day?
3 _____ sugar is there in these sweets?
4 _____ tea have you got?
5 _____ stars can you see in the sky?
6 _____ tomatoes are there in this sandwich?

E Listen and circle.

1 ⟨20⟩ / 30
2 15 / 50
3 60 / 70
4 80 / 90
5 10 / 100

F Say.

10 20 30 40 50 60 70 80 90 100

jam

fizzy drink

pizza

chips

send
Have a great party!

A Read.

E-mail

New   Reply   Forward   Print   Delete   Send & Receive

Hi Sandy,

How are you? I'm fine.

So you're having a party! Here are some ideas for party food and drinks.

Pizza is great food for a party. Sandwiches and chips are also good. I like fizzy drinks, but my sister doesn't like them. The birthday cake must be big! My brother loves cake. Mum makes a chocolate cake with jam for him every Saturday. There are sweets on it too.

Have a great party!

Send me some photos.

Ben

B Answer.

1 Is Ben fine?   Yes

2 Who is having a party?   _____

3 Does Ben's sister like fizzy drinks?   _____

4 What does Ben's brother love?   _____

5 What's on the cake?   _____

C Look and learn.

I'm making a cake for you.

I love it!

me	us
you	you
him	them
her	
it	

Are they at the party? I can't see them.
Look at him. He's sleeping.

D Write.

1 Where are Harry and Mark? Can you see ___them___?
2 This pizza is yummy. Everybody likes _____ .
3 Hi Joe. I'm sending _____ an email.
4 It's Carol's birthday today. Let's buy _____ a present!
5 We're hungry. Please make _____ some sandwiches, Mum.
6 I'm dancing. Look at _____!

E Say.

Please buy some pizza, fizzy drinks and a cake for the party. Thanks.

F Write.

Hi _____,

Please buy _____

_____

_____

for the party.

Thanks,

_____

55

Let's remember!

A Find and stick.

| 1 | 2 | 3 | 4 | 5 | 6 |

hotel   camping   waterfall   village   sleeping bag   library

B Write.

baseball cap   ~~lemonade~~   orange juice   pizza
sandwich   burgers   team   trainers   water

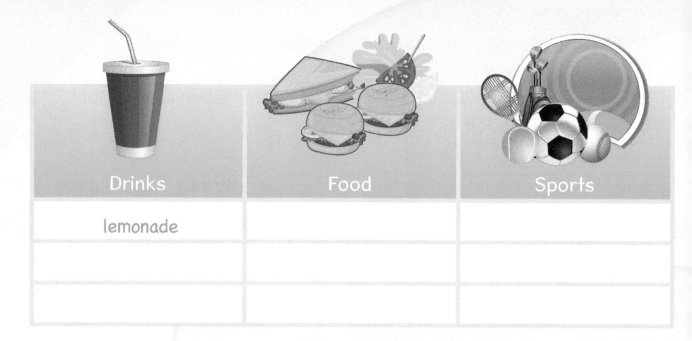

Drinks	Food	Sports
lemonade		

C Circle.

1 The book is on the first grass / (shelf)
2 One hundred is a month / number.
3 We've got thirty / third chips.
4 I'm throwing the ball and Mary is catching / falling it.
5 Canada is a big library / country.
6 The baby is sleeping. Shh / Whee! Be quiet!
7 Can you speak / stay French?
8 My birthday is in summer. It's in January / August.

D Write.

1 I _____'m sending_____ (send) an email.

2 _____ you _____ (have) fun? Yes, we _____ .

3 You _____ (eat) ice!

4 Lynn _____ (not stay) at a hotel.

5 _____ the cat _____ (sleep)? No, it _____ .

6 Hooray! They _____ (win)!

E Write can, can't, must or mustn't.

He ___can___ snowboard.

Shh! You _____ speak!

Mum _____ catch the ball.

It's freezing! I _____ wear a scarf.

She _____ ski.

Dad, _____ I have a toy?
No, you _____ .

F Choose a or b.

1 We're riding a rollercoaster. _____!
   (a) Look at us   b Look at me

2 Be careful! _____ fall on the ice!
   a Let's   b Don't

3 How _____ children are there in the classroom?
   a many   b much

4 These boots are warm. I like _____ .
   a it   b them

5 Sorry! There isn't _____ jam.
   a some   b any

A Find the months.

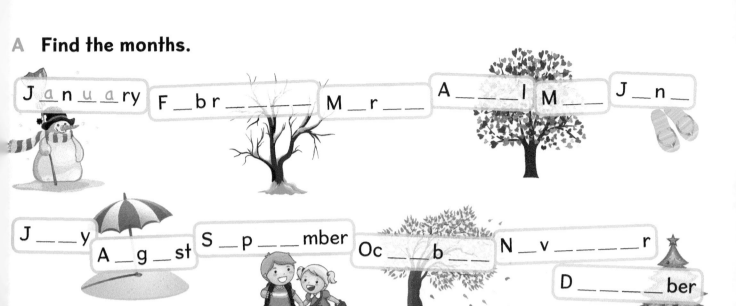

January F _ b r _ _ _ _ _ M _ r _ _ _ A _ _ _ _ l M _ _ _ J _ n _

J _ _ _ y A _ g _ st S _ p _ _ _ mber Oc _ _ _ b _ _ _ N _ v _ _ _ _ _ r D _ _ _ _ _ ber

B Sing.

100 chips are in the kitchen.
100 chips are in the kitchen.
20 boys come in and eat 20 chips.
So there are 80 chips in the kitchen.

60 chips are in the kitchen.
60 chips are in the kitchen.
20 Dads come in and eat 20 chips.
So there are 40 chips in the kitchen.

80 chips are in the kitchen.
80 chips are in the kitchen.
20 girls come in and eat 20 chips.
So there are 60 chips in the kitchen.

40 chips are in the kitchen.
40 chips are in the kitchen.
20 Mums come in and eat 20 chips.
So there are 20 chips in the kitchen.

20 chips are in the kitchen.
20 chips are in the kitchen.
20 dogs come in and eat 20 chips.
So there aren't any chips in the kitchen!

C Make.

1   2   3   4

England

7 Happy Trails in England

cook   doctor   photographer   postman   biscuit   give

A Listen and read.

1 Look! A DVD from the postman!

That's my DVD! Give it to me!

2 Cool! The reporters are in England.

3 Brighton is nice. Look! There's a photographer!

What time is it, Mia?

It's 12 o'clock.

4 Hello children!

Hello reporters! We love your DVDs!

We watch them at school every morning.

5 Look! It's Dina and Ty!

Oh no!

Whee!

6 I want a doctor!

Have a biscuit. My mum makes them. She's a cook.

7 What do you do in the afternoon, Ty?

I eat biscuits!

What time is it, Mia?

It's half past four. Let's go!

B Look and learn.

Mum makes biscuits every day.

And we eat biscuits every day!

I play
you play
he/she/it plays
we/you/they play

Remember!
ride = rides
go = goes
watch = watches

She goes to school in the morning.
They study at night.

C Write.

go   eat   read   ride   ~~want~~   watch

1 I'm hungry. I ___want___ a sandwich.
2 Sally _____ her bike on Saturday.
3 We _____ apples every day.
4 I _____ lots of books on holiday.
5 He _____ DVDs in the afternoon.
6 They _____ to school at 8 o'clock.

Say it!

Listen and say.
be**a**ch
wa**t**ch

Read and listen.
There are sandwiches and chips in the kitchen.

D Listen and tick (✔).

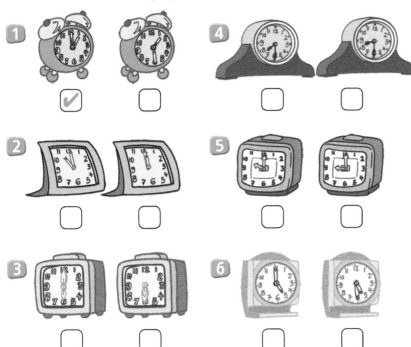

1 ✔ ☐
2 ☐ ☐
3 ☐ ☐
4 ☐ ☐
5 ☐ ☐
6 ☐ ☐

E Say.

What time is it?

It's half past two.

Lesson 2

bow arrow excited scared teach have a lesson

A Listen and read.

Tim is 11 years old. He lives in Africa with his family.

Tim is having a cool lesson. His teacher's name is Nuru. He's a nice man. He's teaching Tim a sport.

Nuru doesn't give his pupils pens or pencils. He gives them a bow and an arrow. This is Tim's first lesson. He's excited, but he's scared too. It's OK. Nuru is a good teacher.

B Choose a or b.

1 The boy's name is
  a Nuru.
  b Tim.

2 Nuru doesn't give his pupils
  a pens and pencils.
  b bows and arrows.

3 In his first lesson, Tim is
  a excited and scared.
  b scared.

4 Nuru is a good
  a teacher.
  b pupil.

C Look and learn.

Dad doesn't like bows and arrows!

I don't dance
you don't dance
he/she/it doesn't dance
we/you/they don't dance

Remember!
don't = do not
doesn't = does not

He doesn't teach children.
You don't like fish.

D Write.

1 I _____don't watch_____ (not watch) TV in the morning.

2 We _____ (not go) to the park every day.

3 Julie _____ (not have) a maths lesson today.

4 My brothers _____ (not play) the guitar.

5 Ron _____ (not want) to play.

6 Dad _____ (not buy) apples at the supermarket.

E Sing.

We are excited!
Yes, we are.
We aren't scared!
No, we aren't.

We are scared.
Yes, we are.
We aren't excited.
No, we aren't.

Hip hip hooray!
Today is a great day.
Hip hip hooray!
Today is a great day.

Oh no! We can't stay.
Today isn't a great day!
Oh no! We can't stay.
Today isn't a great day!

7 What do you want to be?

Lesson 3

actor astronaut firefighter pilot police officer vet

fly

A Read.

Milly: My dad is a pilot.

Jack: Cool. Does he fly every day?

Milly: No, he doesn't.

Jack: I want to be an astronaut or a firefighter.
What do you want to be?

Milly: A vet. I like helping animals.

Jack: My uncle is a vet.

Milly: My uncle is an actor. He's a police officer on TV.

Jack: Do you watch TV at night?

Milly: Yes, we do. We watch my uncle every night.

Jack: I don't like watching TV.

B Write M for Milly or J for Jack.

1 My dad is a pilot. ☐ M
2 I like helping animals. ☐
3 My uncle is a vet. ☐
4 My uncle is an actor. ☐
5 I don't like watching TV. ☐

66

C Look and learn.

Do I watch ...?
Yes, I do.
No, I don't.

Do you watch ...?
Yes, you do.
No, you don't.

Does he/she/it watch ...?
Yes, he/she/it does.
No, he/she/it doesn't.

Do we watch ...?
Yes, we do.
No, we don't.

Do you watch ...?
Yes, you do.
No, you don't.

Do they watch ...?
Yes, they do.
No, they don't.

Does she work in a café? Yes, she does.
Do they play the piano at night? No, they don't.

D Write.

1 ____Do____ you like shopping? Yes, ____I do____ .

2 _____ your friends play tennis at the weekend? No, _____ .

3 _____ Emma go to the park on Friday? Yes, _____ .

4 _____ we listen to music in the afternoon? Yes, _____ .

5 _____ he swim in the winter? No, _____ .

E Say.

I'm Katy. I like making cakes. I want to be a cook.

F Draw and write.

I'm _____ .
I like _____ .
I want _____ .

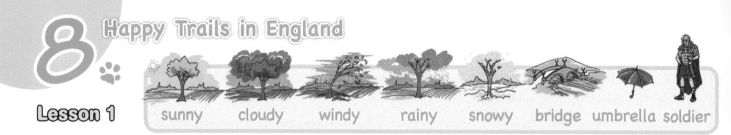

sunny   cloudy   windy   rainy   snowy   bridge   umbrella   soldier

A Listen and read.

1

This is a very old wall.

It's very long too.

It's sunny today. That's good for photos.

2

Look! Soldiers!

Oh no! It's cloudy now!

3

I'm a soldier.

I'm a soldier too!

You're funny!

4

Later ...

We're in Newcastle. Look at that bridge.

Oh no! It's a rainy day now!

It's often rainy in England.

5

I've always got my umbrella.

It's very windy for an umbrella!

It's sometimes windy in Morocco.

6

It's windy and it's rainy.

Oh no!

But it isn't snowy!

It's never snowy in Morocco!

68

B Look and learn.

I've always got an umbrella with me.

I've never got an umbrella.

always	—☐—☐—☐—☐—
often	—☐—☐—☐—☐—
sometimes	—☐—☐—☐—☐—
never	—☐—☐—☐—☐—

Look!

I **always** watch TV in the evening.
It is **often** rainy in England.

C Write.

1 It is snowy in some countries. (never)

   <u>It is never snowy in some countries.</u>

2 We play in the park. (often)

   _____

3 It is windy next to the sea. (sometimes)

   _____

4 I have fun on my holiday. (always)

   _____

5 Ben goes to bed at 10 o'clock. (never)

   _____

D Sing.

It's a sunny day.
Let's go to the park and play.
It's a sunny day.
Come on everybody!

It's a cloudy day.
It's cold out there.
It's a cloudy day.
Look at the sky everybody!

It's a rainy day.
It's wet out there.
It's a rainy day.
Take your umbrellas everybody!

It's a windy day.
Hats fly away.
It's a windy day.
Hold your hats everybody!

It's a snowy day!
Let's go out and play. Hooray!
It's a snowy day.
Come on everybody!

8 Winter is nicer than summer.

Lesson 2

button　head　kids　snowman

A Listen and read.

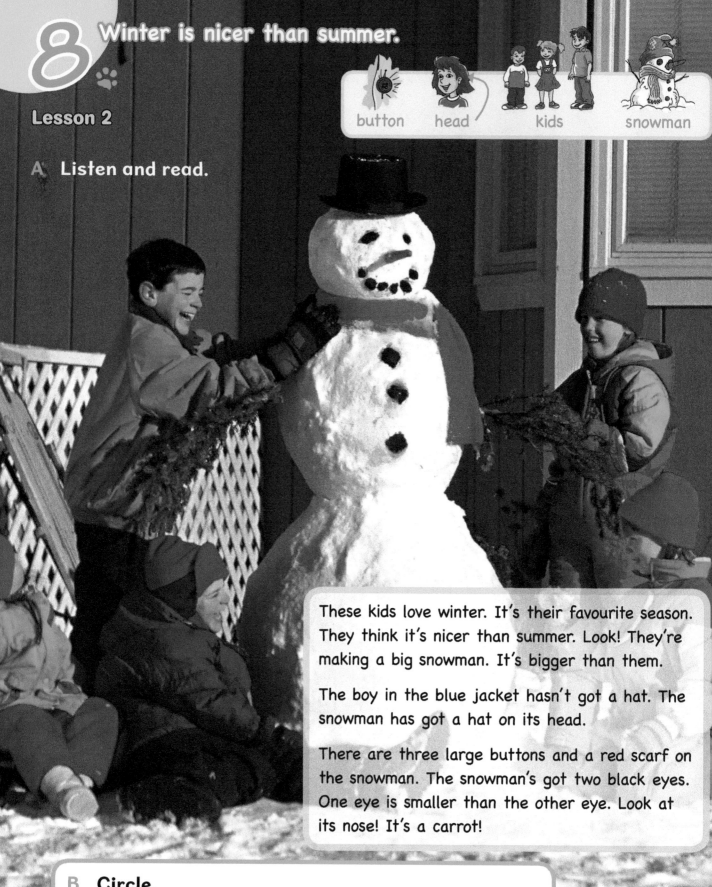

These kids love winter. It's their favourite season. They think it's nicer than summer. Look! They're making a big snowman. It's bigger than them.

The boy in the blue jacket hasn't got a hat. The snowman has got a hat on its head.

There are three large buttons and a red scarf on the snowman. The snowman's got two black eyes. One eye is smaller than the other eye. Look at its nose! It's a carrot!

B Circle.

1　The kids love (winter) / summer.
2　The snowman is bigger / smaller than the kids.
3　The boy isn't wearing a jacket / hat.
4　There's a hat / scarf on the snowman's head.
5　The snowman's nose is a button / carrot.

C Look and learn.

My hat is bigger than your hat!

My hat is nicer than your hat!

warm	warmer
nice	nicer
fat	fatter
happy	happier

good	better
bad	worse

Luke's cat is fatter than Bill's cat.
These trainers are worse than those trainers.

D Write.

1 John is ___thinner than___ (thin) his brother.
2 I'm _____ (lucky) you are.
3 These pupils are _____ (good) those pupils.
4 A leopard's tail is _____ (long) a cat's tail.
5 The blue buttons are _____ (small) the red buttons.

E Listen and tick (✔) Yes or No.

Vicky   Sissy   Dan   May   Bill

		Yes	No
1	May		✔
2	Sissy		
3	Vicky		
4	Dan		
5	Bill		

 Say it!

Listen and say.
head
season

Read and listen.
Dean is wearing his new sweater on the beach.

F Say.

This snowman is bigger than that snowman.

8 It's the smallest animal.

Lesson 3

hand   large   little   scary   sleepy

world
dangerous

A Read.

This is the best poster in our classroom.

Cool animals!

1

This shark is the largest fish. It's larger than a bus! But it's not dangerous.

2
This bird is very little. It's the smallest bird in the world. It's smaller than your hand.

3

Koalas are sleepy animals. They're the sleepiest animals.

4

Giraffes are very tall. They're the tallest animals in the world.

5

This is a spider. Some people think it's scary. What animal do you think is the scariest?

B Write.

bird   giraffe   koala   spider   ~~shark~~

1 It's the biggest fish.   _____shark_____
2 It's the smallest animal.   _____
3 It's the sleepiest animal.   _____
4 It's the tallest animal.   _____
5 It's scary.   _____

72

C Look and learn.

I think my fish is the best pet.

My cat thinks your fish is the yummiest pet!

tall	the tallest
scary	the scariest
big	the biggest
nice	the nicest
good	the best
bad	the worst

Giraffes have got the longest legs.
Jack is the tallest boy in his school.

D Write.

1   This is _____the smallest_____ (small) penguin.
2   Sharks are _____ (scary) fish.
3   Sally is _____ (good) pupil in my school.
4   Are elephants _____ (large) animals?
5   Flies are _____ (bad) insects.
6   I'm not _____ (young) child in my family.

E Say.

This is a whale. It's the biggest animal. I think it's the best animal.

F Draw and write.

This is _____.

It's _____.

I think it's _____.

big wheel   bookshop   bone   clock   dinosaur   museum   queen

yesterday
That's right!

A Listen and read.

1. Yesterday it was rainy, but today it's sunny.
   Look at that big clock.
   That's Big Ben.

2. That bus ride was fun.
   Look! A big wheel!
   It's the London Eye.

3. There's Big Ben. We were there!

4. This is a big museum.
   It's got animals, flowers, rocks and a lot more!

5. This is a dinosaur, Dina.
   No, Ty. This was a dinosaur. Now it's bones!
   Let's go to the bookshop.

6. This dinosaur was a Ty ... Tyran ...
   A Tyrannosaurus rex!
   That's right!

7. That's the Queen's house, Trek!
   Bye.
   Thanks reporters. England is amazing!

B Look and learn.

I was   we were

you were   you were

he was
she was   ⎤→ they were
it was

I was at the museum yesterday.
Dinosaurs were big animals.

C Write was or were.

1 Abby ___was___ excited on the rollercoaster.

2 I _____ at the bookshop yesterday.

3 That old clock _____ my grandmother's.

4 He _____ scared on the big wheel.

5 They _____ at the theatre yesterday.

6 We _____ at school on Monday.

 Say it!

Listen and say.
right
big

Read and listen.
The lion king and the white tiger swim in spring.

D Listen and match.

1 Katy   a rollercoaster
2 Grandma   b museum
3 Dad   c big wheel
4 cousins   d bookshop
5 Mum   e park

E Say.

I was in the park yesterday.

75

T-rex was very dangerous.

friendly earth plant meat sharp

learn
terrible
a long time ago

A **Listen and read.**

These kids are at a museum. They're learning about dinosaurs. Dinosaur means terrible lizard. Dinosaurs were on earth a long time ago. There weren't any people then.

This scary dinosaur was a Tyrannosaurus rex. T-rex wasn't friendly. It was very dangerous. Its head was big and its teeth were sharp. Its food was meat.

Some dinosaurs were little. Their food was plants. There were dinosaurs with wings too.

B **Tick (✔) Yes or No.**

		Yes	No
1	The kids are learning about lizards.	☐	✔
2	T-rex was a dangerous dinosaur.	☐	☐
3	Its teeth were sharp.	☐	☐
4	Its food was plants.	☐	☐
5	Some dinosaurs were small.	☐	☐

C Look and learn.

I wasn't   we weren't
you weren't   you weren't
he wasn't   they weren't
she wasn't
it wasn't

wasn't = was not
weren't = were not

Donna wasn't at school yesterday.
They weren't happy.

T-rex wasn't pink, Amber!

D Write **wasn't** or **weren't**.

1 I _____wasn't_____ at the cinema.

2 We _____ at the library yesterday.

3 Cindy's toys _____ on the shelf.

4 That dog _____ friendly.

5 My cousin _____ in his bedroom.

6 My brother and I _____ in the park.

E Sing.

Dino the dinosaur was very sad.
He wasn't happy at all.
His friends were all big and strong.
But he was small, small, small.

Little Dino the dinosaur,
He was the smallest dinosaur of all!
Little Dino the dinosaur,
He was the cutest dinosaur of all!

One day T-rex was in the forest.
He was there behind a tree.
He was big and scary!
And he was very hungry!

Little Dino was small and fast.
He quickly climbed a tree.
Poor T-rex was hungry all day.
But little Dino got away!

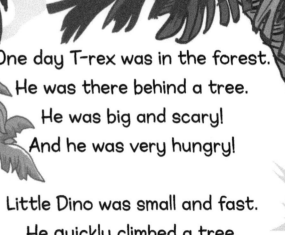

77

9 Cavemen were hunters.

caveman   dark   history   home   strong

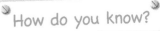
How do you know?

A Read.

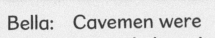

Bella: Cavemen were big and strong!

Dean: They were hunters.

Bella: Were they dinosaur hunters?

Dean: No, they weren't! There weren't any dinosaurs then.

Bella: How do you know?

Dean: We have history lessons at school.

Bella: Was your lesson about cavemen?

Dean: Yes, it was. Their food was meat and plants.

Bella: Were their homes nice?

Dean: No, they weren't. Their homes were caves.

Bella: Was it cold in the caves?

Dean: No, it wasn't. There was a small fire in the cave. But it was dark.

Bella: You know a lot about cavemen, Dean!

B Write.

1 Cavemen were big and ___strong___ .
2 Dean has _____ lessons at school.
3 Cavemen's food was _____ and plants.
4 Their homes were _____ .
5 It wasn't _____ in the cave.
6 It was _____ in the cave.

C Look and learn.

Was your dog wet?

Yes, it was!

Was I ...?	Were **we** ...?
Yes, I was.	Yes, we were.
No, I wasn't.	No, we weren't.
Were **you** ...?	Were you ...?
Yes, you were.	Yes, you were.
No, you weren't.	No, you weren't.
Was he/she/it ...?	Were they ...?
Yes, he/she/it was.	Yes, they were.
No, he/she/it wasn't.	No, they weren't.
Was he in the village?	Were you scared?
Yes, he was.	No, we weren't.

D Write.

1 ___Were___ you at school yesterday? Yes, we ___were___ .

2 _____ they at the theatre yesterday? No, they _____ .

3 _____ the history lesson fun? No, it _____ .

4 _____ Grandpa a tall boy? No, he _____ .

5 _____ you sad yesterday? Yes, I _____ .

6 _____ Mum and Dad at the bookshop? Yes, they _____ .

E Say.

Was your dinosaur strong?

Yes, it was. **It was** big **and** scary. **But it wasn't** fast.

F Draw and write.

This is my dinosaur.

It was _____ and _____ .

But it wasn't _____ .

79

Let's remember!

A Find and stick.

[1]	[2]	[3]	[4]	[5]	[6]
clock	actor	bridge	photographer	vet	big wheel

B Match.

excited
dangerous
large
little

scared
sleepy
friendly
strong

C Write.

3 S

1 B
O
N
E

2 C

4 D

5 P

6 P

D Write.

1 We _____like_____ (like) meat.

2 I _____ (not read) scary books.

3 He always _____ (get up) at 7 o'clock.

4 Sheila _____ (not eat) breakfast on Saturday.

5 _____ you often _____ (go) to the bookshop?

6 _____ Mr Smith _____ (teach) English?

7 Do they go home at 2 o'clock? Yes, they _____ .

8 Does she watch DVDs? No, she _____ .

E Circle.

1 T-rex was the scarier / (scariest) dinosaur.

2 John is the stronger / strongest boy in our school.

3 My cat's teeth are sharper / sharpest than your teeth.

4 The cook here makes the better / best food!

5 Kelly is friendlier / friendliest than Lara.

6 This is the worse / worst museum in the world!

F Write.

1 It _____was_____ cloudy and cold yesterday.

2 I _____ at school yesterday.

3 _____ Jim at the theatre on Saturday? _____ .

4 _____ Mum and the baby sleepy? _____ .

5 There _____ any biscuits.

6 Billy _____ scared of the insect.

Fun and Games

These kids were with their mum in the park yesterday. They were under a large umbrella. It wasn't sunny, but it was fun.

Quiz time!

Look! It's
a rainy.
b snowy.

A Draw, write and colour.

cook   doctor   firefighter   pilot

1

doctor

2

_____

3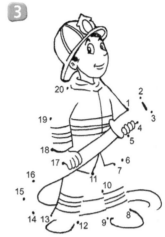

_____

4

_____

B Sing.

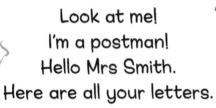

Look at me!
I'm a teacher!
Hello children.
It's time for a lesson!

Look at me!
I'm a postman!
Hello Mrs Smith.
Here are all your letters.

Look at me!
I'm a pilot!
Goodbye England.
Let's fly to Canada.

Look at me!
I'm an astronaut!
Goodbye earth.
I'm going, going to the moon.

C Make.

1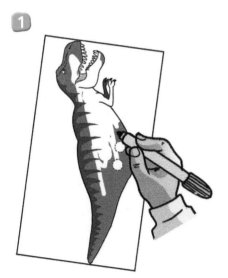

2

3

10 Happy Trails in Japan

 heavy restaurant building suitcase rice

close
pack

A Listen and read.

Later...

86

B Look and learn.

I closed your suitcase, Amber.

Oh no!

I jumped	we jumped
you jumped	you jumped
he jumped	they jumped
she jumped	
it jumped	

like = liked
stop = stopped
study = studied

Yesterday Mum cooked rice.

C Write.

close	like	listen	pack	study	watch

1 Yesterday we __listened__ to music.
2 I _____ the window. It was cold in here.
3 They _____ for their history lesson.
4 You _____ a DVD about Japan.
5 He _____ a lot of clothes in his suitcase.
6 I _____ the food at the restaurant.

Say it!

Listen and say.
city
restaurant
suitcase

Read and listen.
There are ten cinemas and ten restaurants in the city.

D Sing.

What can I eat in Japan?
Can I have ice cream or jam?
I don't know what to do!
What can I eat in Japan?

What can I eat in Greece?
Can I eat rice or fish?
I don't know what to do!
What can I eat in Greece?

Come on, everybody! Let's eat together!
Food from around the world!
Sandwiches, pizzas and rice.
Ice cream, jam and chocolate cake.
Come on, everybody! Let's eat together!
Food from around the world!

87

 desert  pyramid build last week

A Listen and read.

Asim lives in a village in Egypt. His village is near the Nile. It's the longest river in the world.

Last week Asim went to the desert. He saw a small pyramid. A long time ago, people built pyramids in the desert. He saw drawings of cats on the walls in the pyramid.

Yesterday Asim caught some fish in the Nile and he gave one to his cat, Jasmine. Jasmine ate it all. Head, tail and bones!

B Write.

1 Asim lives in a ____village____ .
2 The Nile is the longest _____ in the world.
3 Last week Asim saw a small pyramid in the _____ .
4 Jasmine is a _____ .
5 Jasmine ate a _____ .

C Look and learn.

I caught three fish and you ate them!

I/you/he/she/it went
we/you/they went

build = built   get up = got up
buy = bought   give = gave
catch = caught   go = went
eat = ate   see = saw

We saw a large pyramid.

D Write.

1 Bob's parents ____built____ (build) a house on an island.

2 We _____ (get up) at 8 o'clock yesterday.

3 Mum _____ (give) me a puppy for my birthday.

4 Jack _____ (catch) a butterfly last night.

5 I _____ (go) to the cinema with my family on Saturday.

6 My grandma _____ (buy) a new car.

E Listen and circle.

1 Pete gave a hat to (Joe) / Ann.

2 Tom went to Japan / Egypt last summer.

3 Mary caught one / two big fish.

4 Jack gave Emma a big / small bag.

5 Andrew was in the park / at home yesterday.

F Say.

Last summer I went to a little village. I saw lots of cats. I ate lots of fish too.

10 He's a great player.

Lesson 3

 American
 English
 Greek
 Japanese
 Spanish
 gold medal

A Read.

famous
player
the Olympics

1 Vasilis Spanoulis is Greek. He played basketball for a Greek team in 1998. He was only 16. He went to America, but he didn't stay there. He's in Greece now. He's a great player.

2 David Beckham is English. He plays football. He didn't want to be a doctor or a firefighter. He went to a football school.

3 Ichiro Suzuki is Japanese. He plays baseball. He's very famous in Japan. Ichiro was the first Japanese player in an American baseball team.

4 Rafael Nadal is Spanish. He's a tennis player. He won a gold medal at the Olympics in China. He was amazing!

B Circle.

1 Vasilis Spanoulis didn't stay in Greece / (America).
2 David Beckham isn't English / Spanish.
3 Ichiro Suzuki is from Japan / China.
4 Rafael Nadal plays tennis / basketball.

C Look and learn.

Ouch!

Sorry! I didn't see you there!

I didn't go   we didn't go
you didn't go   you didn't go
he didn't go   they didn't go
she didn't go
it didn't go

We didn't play ice hockey.

D Write.

1 He bought a baseball cap.

    He didn't buy a baseball cap.

2 They went to the bookshop.

_____

3 Katy gave me a computer game.

_____

4 I liked the DVD about the Olympics.

_____

5 John got up at 9 o'clock yesterday.

_____

6 The Spanish team won.

_____

E Say.

This is Wayne Rooney. He's English. He plays football.

F Draw and write.

This is _____ .

_____ .

_____ .

Lesson 1

 sign

train

train station

cross the road

go straight ahead

turn left

turn right

Of course!

A Listen and read.

1 Can you tell me the way to the train station, please?

Of course! Go straight ahead. Then turn left.

2 Look at this train!

It's the fastest train in the world.

3 Look! Mount Fuji. There's snow.

4 Later ...

Tokyo is cool!

Look at all those signs.

Did you pack the map?

Oh no! I didn't.

5 Can you tell me the way to a karaoke café?

Yes. Cross the road and then turn right. There's a karaoke party for kids there today.

6 Happy Trails! Happy Trails! Hello everybody at Happy Trails! ...

Karaoke is fun!

B Look and learn.

Did you study?

No, we didn't.

Did **I** go? Yes, I **did**. No, I **didn't**.	Did **we** go? Yes, we **did**. No, we **didn't**.
Did **you** go? Yes, you **did**. No, you **didn't**.	Did **you** go? Yes, you **did**. No, you **didn't**.
Did **he/she/it** go? Yes, he/she/it **did**. No, he/she/it **didn't**.	Did **they** go? Yes, they **did**. No, they **didn't**.
Did **you** see the sign? Yes, I **did**.	Did **they** sing? No, they **didn't**.

C Write.

1 Did Bill pack the map? (✗)   _No, he didn't._

2 Did we ride our scooter yesterday? (✔) _____

3 Did you do your homework? (✗) _____

4 Did your dog eat the pizza? (✗) _____

5 Did Mum and Dad go to the train station? (✔) _____

D Listen and write.

1 restaurant   _b_

2 café   _____

3 train station   _____

4 library   _____

5 museum   _____

E Say.

Can you tell me the way to the train station?

Of course! Go straight ahead. Turn right and cross the road.

11 They saved its life.

 cage   call   free   ill   open   seal

life
save
find = found
look after

A Listen and read.

Last week Simon and Mary found a baby seal on the beach. It didn't have a mum. It was hungry and thirsty. It was ill too. The children called a vet.

The vet looked after the seal. He gave the seal food and milk.

Today the seal is going to go home. Simon and Mary are on the beach. They are opening the cage. Look! The baby seal is coming out. It's going to be free. The children and the vet saved its life.

B Write.

1   Did the baby seal have a mum?
    No, it didn't.

2   Was the seal hungry and thirsty?
    _____

3   Did the vet look after the seal?
    _____

4   Did the children and the vet save its life?
    _____

C Look and learn.

I'm going to save its life!

I'm going to buy a new T-shirt.

I'm going to play
you're going to play
he's going to play
she's going to play
it's going to play
we're going to play
you're going to play
they're going to play

We're going to see Grandma on Sunday.

D Write.

1 He ___'s going to___ play football.

2 I _____ look after the kitten.

3 We _____ watch TV.

4 The vet _____ save its life.

5 They _____ make a snowman.

6 Our friends _____ go to the beach.

 Say it!

Listen and say.
free
seal

Read and listen.
We see free seals every week on the beach.

E Sing.

There are animals everywhere.
Seals, dolphins, elephants and bears.
Some are ill or have nowhere to stay.
We must help the animals today!
Let's all try to be more green,
Because the forests and seas aren't clean.

Save our animals!
Penguins and pandas.
Meerkats and whales.
Together we must find a way.
Save our animals today!

Save our animals!
Leopards and lions.
Monkeys and frogs.
Together we must find a way.
Save our animals today!

11 Can you help?

clean   dirty   drop litter   plant   nature   start a fire   come

A Read.

SAVE NATURE!

Look at Sunny Beach. It's dirty. Many people drop litter on the beach.

We're going to clean Sunny Beach. It isn't going to be a dirty beach.

Can you help?

Please come to Sunny Beach on:
Saturday 6th April, at 10'clock

We are very sad. Some people started a fire in Windy Forest. There aren't any trees or flowers now. There isn't any food for the animals. We're going to plant trees and have a forest again.

Can you help?

Please come to Windy Forest on:
Sunday 7th April, at 9 o'clock

B Choose a or b.

1 Sunny Beach is
   (a) dirty.   b clean.

2 What do some people do on Sunny Beach?
   a They start a fire.   b They drop litter.

3 When can you help Windy Forest?
   a on 6th April   b on 7th April

4 Where can you help on Sunday?
   a Sunny Beach   b Windy Forest

C Look and learn.

Oh no! Help me clean the rug, Chris.

I'm not going to clean the rug. You can do it!

I'm not going to play
you aren't going to play
he isn't going to play
she isn't going to play
it isn't going to play
we aren't going to play
you aren't going to play
they aren't going to play

He isn't going to drop litter.

D Write.

1 You ___aren't going to ride___ (not ride) your bike in the evening.
2 They _____ (not build) houses in the forest.
3 I _____ (not buy) a new tent.
4 We _____ (not plant) flowers in the garden.
5 The dog _____ (not eat) its food.
6 Meg _____ (not clean) the park on Sunday.

E Say.

I'm going to plant flowers.

I'm not going to drop litter.

F Write.

Save nature!

I'm going to _____ .

_____ .

I'm not _____ .

_____ .

97

12 Happy Trails in Japan

 bark comic draw meet show

 cartoon tomorrow

A Listen and read.

1 A robot show! This is amazing! Are we going to see all the robots?

Yes, we are.

2 I like this dog robot.

Can it bark?

Yes, it can.

Where's Dina?

3

4 Come here and meet Ken. His dad draws cartoons for comics!

5 Are you going to go home tomorrow?

No, we aren't.

Then come to our house!

Later ...

6 These cartoons are for you.

Thank you.

We love Japan! Hooray!

7 My world reporters are the best!

B Look and learn.

Are you going to give me my comic?

No, I'm not. I'm going to read it.

Am I going to play?
Yes, I am.
No, I'm not.

Are you going to play?
Yes, you are.
No, you aren't.

Is he/she/it going to play?
Yes, he/she/it is.
No, he/she/it isn't.

Are we going to play?
Yes, we are.
No, we aren't.

Are you going to play?
Yes, you are.
No, you aren't.

Are they going to play?
Yes, they are.
No, they aren't.

Is he going to stay in a hotel? No, he isn't.
Are they going to see the car show? Yes, they are.

C Write.

1 ___Are___ you going to buy a robot? Yes, ___I am___ .

2 _____ it going to sleep? No, _____ .

3 _____ we going to meet them here? No, _____ .

4 _____ the pupils going to draw? Yes, _____ .

5 _____ Anna going to eat the biscuit? Yes, _____ .

6 _____ you and Ted going to pack your suitcases? No, _____ .

D Listen and choose.

1 Is the girl going to watch TV?
   a Yes, she is.   (b) No, she isn't.

2 Is the boy going to go to the park?
   a Yes, he is.   b No, he isn't.

3 Is Mum going to see the show?
   a Yes, she is.   b No, she isn't.

4 Are they going to sleep?
   a Yes, they are.   b No, they aren't.

5 The girls are going to
   a watch DVDs.   b play computer games.

E Say.

Are you going to watch TV tomorrow?

No, I'm not. I'm going to play basketball.

99

airport   flat   ghost train   passport   postcard

need
tonight
parents

A Listen and read.

My sisters and I will be in America in July for two weeks. My aunt and uncle live there. We'll stay in their flat. It's bigger than our house! Guess what? They'll take us to Disney World!

Tonight we'll pack our suitcases and tomorrow we'll go to the airport. We'll need our passports too.

The little girl in the photo with Mickey Mouse is my cousin, May. We'll see Mickey Mouse too. We'll go on a ghost train! I love scary rides!

My summer holidays will be great. I'll send my parents and friends a postcard.

B Choose a or b.

1   Susan will go to America with
    a her parents.   (b) her sisters.

2   She will stay in America for
    a two weeks.   b all of July.

3   Susan's aunt and uncle have got a
    a house.   b flat.

4   Who is the little girl in the photo?
    a Susan's sister   b Susan's cousin

C Look and learn.

At 2 o'clock the summer holidays will start.

Hooray!

I/you/he/she/it'll go
we/you/they'll go

'll go = will go

I'll send you a postcard.
They will sleep in a tent.

D Write.

cook   go   have   play   ride   send

Hi Dan,

Tomorrow I'll be with my grandma and grandpa.
They live on an island. I (1) _____will go_____ to the
beach with my friends everyday. We
(2) _____ lots of fun. We (3) _____
our bikes too. Grandma (4) _____ my
favourite food and Grandpa (5) _____
tennis with me. I (6) _____ you a postcard.

Bye,

Abby

Say it!

Listen and say.
love
holiday
airport
open

Read and listen.
My brother's
photo in his
passport is scary.

E Chant.

We'll see you in
September, Mr Smith.
We'll see you in
September, Mrs Jones.
We can't stay.
We're on holiday.
So bye bye!
See you later.
Off we go!

Let's do the holiday hop!
Hop on your left foot.
Hop on your right foot.
Then turn left and now
turn right.
Clap your hands.
And jump up high.
Come on, boys and girls!
Let's do the holiday hop!

12 We'll have fun on holiday!

Lesson 3

 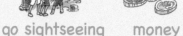

diary   go sightseeing   money   trip   write

hour
take
go shopping

A Read.

1

Ralph, Canada

We always go to the mountains on holiday. I love it there. It's a long trip — five hours in the car! I'll take my MP3 player with me and I'll listen to music.

2

Charlotte, England

In August Mum and I will go to London for three days. We'll go shopping! We won't stop! Grandma gave me some money, so I'll buy lots of clothes.

3

Sammy, Morocco

In spring I'll go on a trip to Greece. It won't be very hot, so we'll go sightseeing. I'll take my camera .

4

Nana, Japan

This summer we won't go on holiday in Japan. We'll go to Australia. I'll take my diary with me. I will write in it every day!

B Circle.

1 Nana / (Ralph) will listen to music.

2 Ralph / Charlotte is from England.

3 Charlotte / Nana likes shopping.

4 Sammy / Ralph will go to Greece.

5 Charlotte / Sammy will go sightseeing.

6 Nana / Sammy will go on a trip in summer.

C Look and learn.

It won't be rainy! It's summer!

I/you/he/she/it/ won't go
we/you/they won't go

won't = will not

He will not come to the party.
We won't go sightseeing on a hot day.

D Write.

1 we / buy / postcards / won't

   We won't buy postcards.

2 trip / go / they / on / won't / a

   _____

3 will / you / sleep / not / in / tent / a

   _____

4 shopping / won't / tomorrow / she / go

   _____

5 I / in / my / won't / every day / diary / write

   _____

E Say.

I won't go shopping in London. I'll go sightseeing.

He won't go shopping in London. He'll go sightseeing.

F Write.

Email

Hi _____ !

How are you?

I'm in _____ .

I'll _____ .

I won't _____ .

Bye for now!

_____

Let's remember!

A Find and stick.

gold medal   airport   suitcase   seal   train   money

B Match.

1 plant   shopping
2 start   litter
3 cross   a fire
4 turn   a tree
5 go   left
6 drop   the road

C Write.

> comics   desert   ghost train   postcard   restaurant   ~~trip~~

1 Our _____trip_____ to America was great.
2 We ate rice at the Japanese _____ .
3 Do you read _____?
4 Please send me a _____ from Japan.
5 The ride on the _____ was very scary!
6 Did you see the pyramids in the _____?

D Circle.

1 I'm hot. Please close / (open) the window.
2 Let's clean / meet the beach. There's litter everywhere.
3 Our cat was very ill / dirty, but the vet saved its life.
4 She sometimes writes in her flat / diary.
5 Where's the new restaurant? Turn / Find right and cross the road.
6 Did lots of people build / bark the pyramids?

E Write.

1 We _____closed_____ (close) the door.
2 He _____ (not study) for the test.
3 They _____ (see) their friends on the train.
4 _____ Sophie _____ (like) the Greek restaurant?
5 We _____ (catch) a big fish in the river.
6 Did you meet Bob at the museum? No, I _____ .

F Match.

1 I'm going   take the train.
2 We're going to   to pack my suitcase.
3 Are you   a cartoon.
4 Is he going   going to watch the Olympics?
5 I'm going to draw   Yes, he is.
6 Is he going to fly?   to write to you?

G Write.

catch   eat   go   listen to   pack   watch

He ____won't go____ sightseeing.

Grandpa _____ TV.

The cat _____ lots of fish.

They _____ chocolate.

She _____ lots of clothes.

The kids _____ to
their MP3 players.

Fun and Games

Kim is from Australia. She went to this fantastic park. She saw many animals. There were koalas, kangaroos, snakes and birds. The animals here are free and they aren't in cages.

Quiz time!

What is the largest egg in the world?

a a canary egg
b an ostrich egg

A Write.

I will save nature!   I will save you, little parrot!

I'm planting a tree.   I'm Superparrot!   Ouch!

1. I'm Superparrot!

2.

3.

B Sing.

We're going to go on a trip,
A trip around the world.
We'll have lots of fun.
We'll talk to everyone,
On our trip around the world.

I'll eat lots of sausages!
I'll have some fish and chips!
I'll watch exciting football games!
I'll go to the Olympics!

I'll swim and play in the cleanest sea!
I'll walk in the warmest rain!
I'll climb the tallest skyscraper!
I'll ride the fastest train!
On our trip around the world!

C Make.

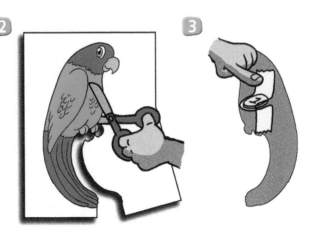

Cinderella

This story is from France.

 Cinderella
 Stepmother
 Trudy and Matilda
 The fairy godmother

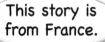

1

You're a good puppy. You are my best friend.

Yap! Yap!

2

This kitchen is messy, Cinderella.

I'm sorry, Stepmother.

I'm thirsty.

I'm hungry.

3

Here you are. Some lemonade and a sandwich.

Yuk!

Come on, girls.

4

An invitation from Prince Phillip. There's a party at the castle.

Hooray! He's very handsome. I want to marry him.

I want to marry him too!

5

We're going to the castle. You can't come, Cinderella.

You haven't got a beautiful dress.

And nice shoes.

6

Cinderella, I'm your fairy godmother. Why are you sad?

There's a party at the castle. But I can't go!

Prince Phillip

The puppy

7

I've got an idea!

Pumpkins and puppies. Shoes and dresses. It's time for a party!

8

Cool! I'm a driver!

Thank you, Fairy Godmother.

But you must leave at 12 o'clock.

9

It's a great party, Prince Phillip.

Thank you. Let's dance.

Who is that girl?

She's ugly!

10

Oh no! It's 12 o'clock!

Don't go! What's your name?

The prince has got her shoe.

We've got a brown puppy too!

11

Later...

This is my shoe.

No, it isn't. Ouch!

Be quiet!

Can I see the shoe, please?

12

This is your shoe. Marry me, Cinderella!

Yes!

Oh no!

Yap! Yap!

Let's sing!

109

Aladdin

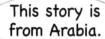

This story is from Arabia.

Aladdin

Jasmine

Jamal

1

I'm Aladdin. You're beautiful. What's your name?

I'm Princess Jasmine.

You mustn't talk to that boy, Jasmine.

2

I'm going to buy Jasmine a present.

We haven't got any money. You must work, Aladdin.

I've got an idea!

3

Please find a job, Aladdin.

OK Mum.

Hello, Aladdin. I can give you a job.

4

Who are you? What is the job?

Erm ... I'm your uncle! I'm looking for a lamp. Can you find it, please? I'll give you lots of money!

5

The lamp is in the cave. Can you see it?

Yes, I can.

6

Give me the lamp now!

No. You're going to leave me here.

Yes, I am! You'll stay here for 100 days!

Help!

110

The genie
 Aladdin's mum
 The sultan
 princess

7
This cave is dark. I'm scared. Hmm ... This lamp is dirty. I'll clean it. What ...?

8
I am the genie of the lamp. I can give you three wishes.

Amazing! 3 wishes? Well, my 1st wish is *I want to go home.*

9
Where were you? Who is your new friend? Did you find a job?

Ouch! Who's this?

She's my mum. Ouch! Mum, meet my genie.

10
I'm sorry! Here's some tea.

I've got 2 wishes now. My 2nd wish is *I want to be a prince.* My 3rd wish is *I want to marry Princess Jasmine.*

Later ...

11
My name is Aladdin. I want to marry Jasmine.

Welcome, Prince Aladdin! Jasmine, do you love Aladdin?

Yes, I do. I'll marry him on Saturday.

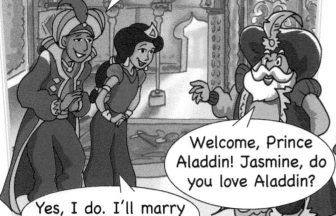

12
Give me the lamp!

No! You're bad!

Thank you, Genie!

Congratulations!

Let's sing!

Halloween

pumpkin   ghost   witch   Trick or treat!

A Read.

Halloween is fun! Children wear scary costumes. They make pumpkin faces and play trick or treat. They go to people's houses and say 'Trick or treat! Have you got any sweets?'

Look at Trisha! She's got a great costume. She's a witch! She likes witch and ghost costumes. She's got a pumpkin. There are a lot of sweets in it. Yummy!

B Match.

1 Children wear scary costumes.
2 They make pumpkin faces.
3 They play trick or treat.
4 She's a witch.

C Colour.

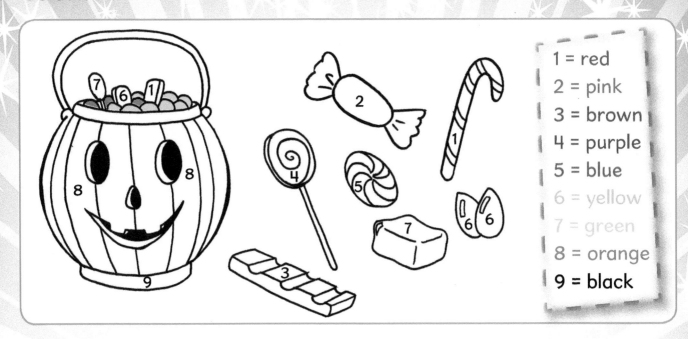

1 = red
2 = pink
3 = brown
4 = purple
5 = blue
6 = yellow
7 = green
8 = orange
9 = black

D Write.

¹C	O	S	T	U	M	E	

²W			

Trick or ...! →

³T				T	

⁴H			L		W		

⁵G				T

⁶P				

Have you got any s _ _ _ _ _ _?

E Make.

1   2   3   4

113

Happy New Year!

midnight   party hats   sparkler   Happy New Year!

A Read.

It's the last day of December. Mum, Dad, Rob and Mel are having a party. They've got party hats and sparklers. It's almost 12 o'clock. Five, four, three, two, one ... Happy New Year! It's midnight! The new year is here! It's now 1st January. Goodbye old year!

Let's sing and dance! Let's have fun!

B Match.

1	It's the last day of	fun!
2	It's almost 12	Year!
3	Happy New	December.
4	It's now 1st	January.
5	Let's have	o'clock.

C How many? Find and write.

I can see _t _ _ _ _ _ _ _ sparklers.

I can see _e _ _ _ _ _ _ _ party hats.

D Tick (✔).

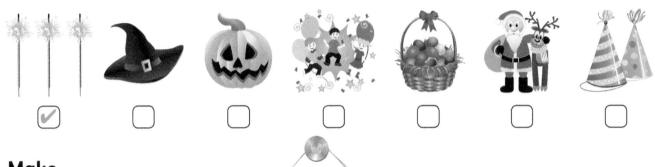

E Make.

This year ...

 Janet   I mustn't shout in the classroom.

 Sandra   I mustn't watch TV all day.

 Mark   I must listen to Mum and Dad.

 George   I mustn't eat lots of sweets.

 Mrs Green   I must walk to school.

May Day

candy floss — fair — parade

A Read.

May 1st is a holiday in many countries. Its name is May Day.

In England, girls wear flowers in their hair. They wear summer dresses and they dance. The nicest girl is the May Queen. Look at Brenda. She's the May Queen and she's beautiful.

In many towns there are parades. There are fairs too. People eat candy floss and they play games.

What do you do on May Day?

B Write.

1 May Day is the first day of _____ .

2 In England girls wear _____ in their hair.

3 The _____ girl is the May Queen.

4 At the fairs people eat _____ _____ .

C Circle.

M	A	Y	D	A	Y	D	C
A	Y	D	A	Q	U	E	A
Y	F	P	Z	F	A	I	N
Q	P	A	R	A	D	E	D
U	H	O	L	I	D	A	Y
E	F	R	X	R	Q	U	F
E	C	A	N	D	F	S	L
N	G	D	D	L	A	N	O
D	F	L	O	W	E	R	S
F	L	O	O	W	R	E	S

D Read and write.

1 I'm a Saturday or a Sunday. I'm a Monday too. I can be a Tuesday, a Wednesday, a Thursday and a Friday. But I'm not a school day. What am I?

h _ _ _ _ _ d _ y

2 I'm beautiful and pink. I live in the garden. You can see me on trees too. What am I?

fl _ _ w _ _ _

3 Sometimes I'm pink. Sometimes I'm white. I can be blue too. You can buy me at the fair. Children like to eat me. What am I?

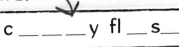

c _ _ _ _ _ y fl _ _ s _

E Make.

117

Leo

Dina

Wonderful World 2 Pupil's Book
Jennifer Heath

Publisher: Jason Mann

Director of Content Development: Sarah Bideleux

Commissioning Editor: Carol Goodwright

Development Editor: Lynn Thomson

Assistant Editor: Manuela Barros

Content Project Editor: Amy Smith

Art Director: Natasa Arsenidou

Cover Designer: Vasiliki Christoforidou

Text Designers: Tania Diakaki, Sophia Ioannidou

Compositor: Dora Danasi

National Geographic Editorial Liaison: Leila Hishmeh

Acknowledgements
Illustrated by: Panagiotis Angeletakis, Spyros Kontis, Theodoros Piakis
Music composed by: Evdoxia Banani, Vagelis Markantonis
Recorded at Motivation Sound Studios and GFS-PRO Studio
Production at GFS-PRO Studio by George Flamouridis

The publisher would like to thank the following sources for permission to reproduce their copyright protected photos: **Getty Images** – pp. 94 (Cyril Ruoso/JH Editorial/Minden Pictures); **Istockphoto** – pp. 15 (Erikas Visakavicius), 18 (Linda Kloosterhof), 23 (Anna Utekhina, Kevin Klopper, Eric Isselee), 65 (Colleen Bradley); **National Geographic** – pp. 12–13 (GUY NEEDHAM), 22 (SKIP BROWN), 28 (JOEL SARTORE), 36–37 (DAVID EDWARDS), 46 (Tim Laman), 52 (John Burcham), 58 (STACY GOLD), 60–61 (SCOTT S. WARREN), 76 (VAN OVERBEEK, WILL), 84–85 (ALISON WRIGHT), 100 (JUSTIN GUARIGLIA), 106 (WINFIELD PARKS); **Photolibrary Group** – pp. 34 (Alaskastock), 70, 82 (Alaskastock), cover (Design Pics Inc); **Photos.com** – p. 57, 102; **Shutterstock** – pp. 16 (Losevsky Pavel), 17 (Suzanne Tucker), 18 (Petrenko Andriy, Stuart Monk, Monkey Business Images) 23 (Medvedev Andrey, Eric Isselée, dusan964), 24 (KULISH VIKTORIIA, Ivica Drusany, photoaloja, David Hernandez), 30 (Monkey Business Images), 33 (Tischenko Irina, Raisa Kanareva, Monkey Business Images, sonya etchison, Rafa Irusta, BestPhoto1), 35 (Pakhnyushcha, Maggie Molloy, travis manley, Shebeko, Joao Virissimo, yantra, studio online, FERNANDO BLANCO CALZADA), 40 (DAWN KISH), 42 (mates), 48 (Dmitriy Shironosov, Vladimir Melnikov), 54 (3445128471, Fotoline, Koksharov Dmitry, paprika), 57 (Andresr, Indigo Fish, Ilya D. Gridnev), 64 (MICHAEL MELFORD), 67 (Jacek Chabraszewski), 72 (Dmitriy Shironosov, Rostislav Ageev, Steve Byland, Walter Quirtmair, Anke van Wyk, Cheryl Casey), 78 (Marilyn Volan), 81 (Alexey Fursov, Adrian Hughes, Losevsky Pavel, Losevsky Pavel, Cecilia Lim H M, Ann Worthy), 88 (V. J. Matthew), 90 (fengzheng), 96 (kots, vso, Mikhail Zahranichny, John Labrentz), 101 (Pablo H Caridad), 102 (Denise Fortado, Zakharoff, Monkey Business Images, Dmitry Nikolajchuk, Raisa Kanareva, sonya etchison, sming, Regisser), 103 (godrick), 104 (sonya etchison), 105 (silver-john, Hallgerd, StockLite).

For permission to use material from this text or product, submit all requests online at **www.cengage.com/permissions**
Further permissions questions can be emailed to
permissionrequest@cengage.com

ISBN: 978-1-111-40203-7

National Geographic Learning
Cheriton House
North Way
Andover
Hampshire
SP10 5BE
United Kingdom

Cengage Learning is a leading provider of customized learning solutions with office locations around the globe, including Singapore, the United Kingdom, Australia, Mexico, Brazil and Japan. Locate your local office at: **international.cengage.com/region**

Cengage Learning products are represented in Canada by Nelson Education, Ltd.

Visit National Geographic Learning online at **ngl.cengage.com**

Visit our corporate website at **www.cengage.com**

Printed in the United Kingdom by Ashford Colour Press
Print Number 13 Print Year 2022

MIX
Paper from responsible sources
FSC® C011748